How High is the Sky?

Edited by Gillian Doherty
With thanks to Dr. Roger Brugge for information about the sky

First published in 2009 by Usborne Publishing Ltd, 83-85 Saffron Hill, London EC1N 8RT, England.
www.usborne.com Copyright © 2009 Usborne Publishing Ltd.

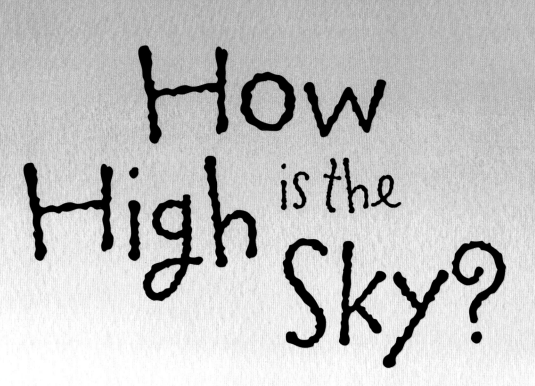

How High is the Sky?

Anna Milbourne

Illustrated by Serena Riglietti

Designed by Laura Wood

Pipkin was a very small penguin
who was always asking
very big questions.

Why are snowflakes cold?

How deep
is the sea?

Does the sun
go to bed
at night?

But the thing he wanted to know most of all was...

"How high
is the sky?"

"Why don't you fly up here
and see for yourself?"
squawked a wandering albatross.

"I'm a penguin," said Pipkin.
"Penguins can't fly."

"Oh dear," said the albatross.
"Well, I'll take you, if you like."

"Yes please," said Pipkin.

They flew up past a flock of birds...

...and up into the blue.

But the sky was much
too high to touch.

"Flying is fun," said Pipkin.
"But I still don't know the answer.
How high IS the sky?"

"I don't know,"
  panted the albatross.
"This is as high as I can go."

"I can go higher," called
a passing hot-air balloonist.
"I'll take you, if you like."

"Yes please," said Pipkin.

They floated up
past some fluffy clouds.

Pipkin tried to catch
one, but his lasso
went right through.

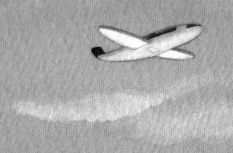

The ground was very far away.
But the sky didn't look
any closer at all.

"Ballooning is wonderful," said Pipkin.
"But I still don't know the answer.
How high IS the sky?"

"I don't know,"
the balloonist shrugged.
"This is as high as I can go."

"I can go higher,"
said a passing astronaut.
"I'll take you, if you like."

"Yes please," said Pipkin.

They flew up and up...   ...and up and up...

...to where the blue turned into deep black space and silver stars shone all around.

They flew on until they reached the moon.

They landed the rocket...

...moonwalked around...

...and looked up at the stars.

"The stars are in the sky too," said Pipkin. "And they're even further than the moon. I still don't know the answer. How high IS the sky?"

"I don't know," said the astronaut.
"This is as high as I can go."

Pipkin was already so high
that he couldn't see his Mama
and he couldn't see his igloo
and he couldn't see the South Pole.

He was ever so far away.

"Perhaps it's time to go home," said Pipkin.

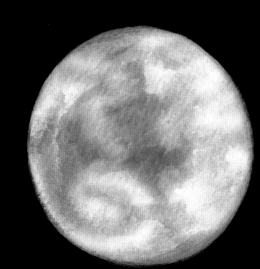

So they did just that.

Pipkin said to his Mama:

"I flew up past the birds
and up past the clouds
and up past the blueness
and all the way to the moon...

...but the sky just kept on going and going."

"I think I know the answer now," said Pipkin.
"The sky goes on forever."

Pipkin's Mama tucked him into bed.
"So that means there's plenty more
to explore another day," she said.

"Sweet dreams, my little Pip."

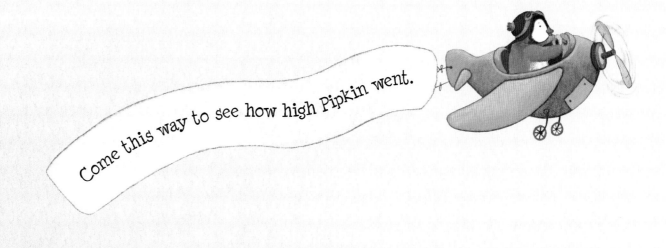

Come this way to see how high Pipkin went.

Open the envelope to see how high Pipkin went.